HAPPY MOTORING!

Canine Life in the Fast Lane

Jon Winokur and Norrie Epstein

Abbeville Press · Publishers

New York · London · Paris

INTRODUCTION

4

To a dog, motoring isn't just a way
of getting from here to there, it's also a thrill and an adventure. The
mere jingle of car keys is enough to send most any dog into a whim-
pering, tail-wagging frenzy. It doesn't matter how often he's been
driven to the kennel or the vet's, his enthusiasm never flags. A dog's
joy in motoring is pure, unselfconscious, and contagious: whenever
we see a motoring dog, it never fails to lift our spirits.

These photographs depict a wide range of canine motoring
styles. Some dogs abandon themselves to ecstasy, noses quivering,
necks stretched to the limit, ears flapping in the wind. Others sit in
stately majesty, allowing themselves to be chauffeured. Some wrig-
gle their snouts through a crack of open window, desperate for

every whiff. Some bark at the passing scenery, others dart frantically from side to side. Even the sedate ones, those who sit like human passengers looking straight ahead, are carefully absorbing the moving feast.

But exactly what is it about dogs and cars? Not only cars but also trains, trucks, vans, pickups, and motorcycles. (Especially motorcycles.) According to one expert, motoring is ideally suited to the canine personality because dogs are eminently convivial creatures, and a motoring dog is assured that he's in on the action and not missing any fun. Motoring with the family is thus the rough equivalent of roaming with the pack. Another explanation is that motorized travel satisfies some primal canine need for swift movement. Or perhaps it's the lure of new and exotic scents. Dogs read the world through their noses, so motoring may be to them what sightseeing is to us: a refreshing (and broadening) break from the humdrum.

No doubt every dog owner has his own explanation for this felicitous phenomenon. The exhilaration of speed, the rhythmic vibration of the engine, the anticipation of going somewhere, anywhere—all may play a part. Perhaps the answer lies deep in the canine spirit. But one thing is clear: almost without exception, dogs love motoring.

Motoring is the ultimate expression
of doggie *joie de vivre.*

Lloyd Ogden, CANINE BEHAVIOR EXPERT

9

Any open car door is an
invitation to get in.

Merrill Markoe

Most dogs love car riding, but to [my beagle] Sam it was a passion that never waned—even in the night hours. He would gently leave his basket when the world was asleep . . . and follow me out into the cold. He would then be on the seat before I got the car door fully open.

James Herriot

13

Every summer, for a week or so, we
baby-sit our friends' dog, Sandy. The dog
is a golden retriever, quite a nice fellow,
who wears his heart on his paw and all
that. The dog enjoys riding in a '68
Mustang convertible so much that he
often runs into the garage and sits
hopefully in the backseat.

Ann Beattie

Dogs LOVE to go for rides.
A dog will happily get into any vehicle
going anywhere.

Dave Barry

My dogs sit up and look out the whole time and notice things, such as game getting up or other dogs on the road side. One little cocker sings during the whole journey.

E. Douglas Wolff

A really companionable and indispensable
dog is an accident of nature. You can't get
it by breeding for it, and you can't buy it
with money. It just happens along.

E. B. White

The great pleasure of a dog is that you may make a fool of yourself with him and not only will he not scold you, but he will make a fool of himself too.

Samuel Butler

To a country vet like myself whose life was spent on the roads and lanes these dogs were very important. The pattern was always the same, Dan stretched on the passenger seat with his head on my knee, Hector peering through the windshield, his paws balanced on my hand as it rested on the gear lever. Dan wasn't worried about what went on outside but Hector hated to miss a thing. His head bobbed around erratically as I changed gear but his feet never slipped off my hand.

James Herriot

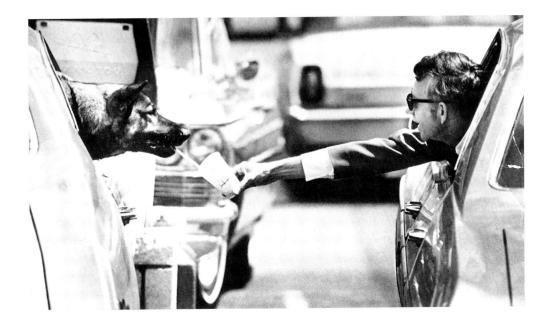

The dog was created specially for children.
He is the god of frolic.

Henry Ward Beecher

40

A dog is like an eternal Peter Pan,
a child who never grows old and who
therefore is always available to
love and be loved.

Aaron Katcher

Mutt enjoyed traveling by car, but he was an unquiet passenger. He suffered from the delusion, common to dogs and small boys, that when he was looking out the right-hand side, he was probably missing something far more interesting on the left-hand side. In addition, he could never be quite sure whether he preferred the front seat—and looking forward—or the rumble seat—and looking backward. . . . Riding in the rumble did strange things to him, and I have a theory that his metabolism was disturbed by the enforced intake of air under pressure from the slip stream, so that he became oxygen drunk. He would grow wild-eyed and, although not normally a drooling dog, he would begin to salivate. Frequently he would stand up with his front feet on the back of Mother's neck, and he would drool on her until, driven to extremes, she would poke him sharply on the chin, whereupon he would mutter, and come back to drool on me.

But his favorite position, when he became really full of oxygen, was to extrude himself gradually over one of the rear mudguards until there was nothing of him remaining in the car except his hind feet and his tail. Here he would balance precariously, his nose thrust far out into the slip stream and his large ears fluttering in the breeze.

Farley Mowat

He may be a dog, but don't tell me he
doesn't have a real grip on life.

Kendall Hailey

An Airedale, erect beside the chauffeur
of a Rolls-Royce,

Often gives you the impression he's there
from choice.

E. B. White

52

The Dark Side of Motoring: waiting in the car while their human is at the cleaners or in the market, they assume the driver's seat out of insecurity. It's the next best thing to having you there. In some cases, there may also be an element of rebelliousness.

Lloyd Ogden, CANINE BEHAVIOR EXPERT

My Scottie refused to go for a walk with a friend of the house, but she would joyously accompany any stranger who drove a car. On one occasion, after she had become totally blind, she escaped from the house and climbed into an immense van which was removing our furniture to another part of the town. She established herself on the driver's seat, and sat there awaiting the departure with an air of ineffable satisfaction.

Mazo de la Roche

A dog, more than any other creature, it seems to me, gets interested in one subject, theme, or object in life, and pursues it with a fixity of purpose which would be inspiring to Man if it were not so troublesome.

E. B. White

63

We had one dog who considered a cross-country trip a perfect way to survey a few thousand miles of hunting country. He wanted his window open so he could keep a nose out there to catch whiffs of quail in Missouri, prairie chickens in Kansas, pheasants in Iowa. It was quite a charge to watch him light up as we passed birdy-looking hedges or draws.

Charles F. Waterman

It was surely not for nothing that Rover is
dog's most common name.

John Galsworthy

When I started driving our old four-door green DeSoto, I always took Skip on my trips around town. He rode with his snout extended far out the window, and if he caught the scent of one of the boys we knew, he would bark and point toward him, and we would stop and give that person a free ride. Skip would shake hands with our mutual friend, and lick him on the face and sit on the front seat between us. Cruising through the fringes of town, I would spot a group of old men standing around up the road. I would get Skip to prop himself up against the steering wheel, his black head peering out of the windshield, while I crouched out of sight under the dashboard. Slowing the car to ten or fifteen, I would guide the steering wheel with my right hand while Skip, with his paws, kept it steady. As we drove by the Blue Front Café, I could hear one of the men shout: "Look at that ol' dog drivin' a car!"

Willie Morris

Number one way life would be different
if dogs ran the world:

All motorists must drive with
head out of window!

David Letterman

Considering what they have to put up with, dogs have made remarkable adjustments to traveling on wheels. Wise owners have learned not to interfere with the dog's enjoyment of the trip; they let him be himself—a dog.

Stephen Baker

Photo Credits

To Reid Boates

ACKNOWLEDGMENTS

We wish to thank John Browner, Patricia Fabricant, Celia Fuller, Nancy Grubb, Dede Hatch, Eve Karlin, Myrna Smoot, Laura Straus, Martha Tabor, and Baron Wolman for their invaluable contributions. We're especially indebted to Gillian Speeth for her resourcefulness and good humor.

EDITOR: Nancy Grubb
DESIGNER: Celia Fuller
PRODUCTION EDITOR: Jeffrey Golick
PRODUCTION MANAGER: Lou Bilka

First edition

2 4 6 8 10 9 7 5 3 1

Library of Congress Cataloging-in-Publication Data
Winokur, Jon.
Happy motoring! : canine life in the fast lane / Jon Winokur and Norrie Epstein.
p. cm.
ISBN 0-7892-0286-7
1. Dogs—Behavior. 2. Dogs—Transportation. I. Epstein, Norrie II. Title.
SF433.W56   1997
779'.329772—dc21   97-5306